Poems

BY

RALPH J. TAYLOR

Order this book online at www.trafford.com
or email orders@trafford.com

Most Trafford titles are also available at major online book retailers.

Printed in the United States of America.

ISBN: 978-1-4269-7957-6 (sc)
ISBN: 978-1-4269-8206-4 (e)

Library of Congress Control Number: 2011913071

Trafford rev. 11/08/2011

 www.trafford.com

North America & international
toll-free: 1 888 232 4444 (USA & Canada)
phone: 250 383 6864 ♦ fax: 812 355 4082

This book is dedicated to my good friend Dr. Henry C. Frisby, Ph.D. who inspired me to start writing poetry. Without his prodding I never would have. He steered me in the right direction. Then there is Alice, my wife, who would review my work and suggest corrections. Most of all there is God who put the words in my head in order that I might put them down on paper.

DO YOU?

When the sun comes up
Just look around
What do you see?
It is nature that has a bound

Do you see the flowers?
Growing from the ground
Do you see the trees?
With all their leaves surround

Do you see the lake?
With the water so blue
Do you see the ducks?
Swimming on the lake too

Do you hear the birds singing?
High up in the tree
They are singing their songs
Yes, for you and me

Do you see the cat?
In the back yard
Trying to climb the tree
And trying real hard

Do you see the dog?
Running in the field
Do you see its owner?
Trying to make it heel

Do you feel the sun?
Shinning on your face
Do you see other people?
All from the human race

Do you feel the breeze?
Blowing on you back
No, you can't deny it
This is a real fact

Can you feel the rain coming?
Coming from the West
It will be a downpour
And create a real big mess

Do you see the sand?
Laying on the beach
The shape of each one is different
For every one and each

Do you see the fire?
With its big red ball
Off in the distance
It makes the trees fall

Do you see the smoke?
Coming from the fire
As you watch it
It just gets higher and higher

Yes my friend I tell you
Open your eyes and really see
Mother Nature is all around us
And she is there for you and me

FIREFLIES

As the cool summer night approaches, the air is filled
with moving colors of yellow and gold.
There is glee in the faces of the children who hurry to
their houses.
They will obtain a jar with holes punched in the lid.
They will return to capture and imprison as many
fireflies as they can.

The little boys believe that by removing the wings of
these insects, they can keep them from flying away.
Therefore, they will look pretty and last a long time
with the jar sitting on their bureau.

How cruel can this be? Does the insect feel the pain
when their wings are so forcefully removed?
Would not this be the same as if we as humans had our
limbs torn from our bodies?

Little do the children realize or know what they have
done to one of God's creations.
All this just so they can look at a jar of blinking lights.

The pleasure is short lived, as soon the little lightning
bugs are dead. Their lights extinguished forever.

Luck

As I was leaving the lottery counter the woman said to me, "Good Luck." What does she know about luck? All I have is bad luck.
My wife just left me, my kids hate me, and my dog got run over yesterday, On top of that I wrecked my truck this morning.

Do I need good luck? You bet I do. Yesterday my boss fired me after being with the company for nineteen and one half years. That means,
"No Pension." On the way out of the office I tripped over a waste basket and broke my arm.

While at the hospital getting a cast put on my arm, the Doctor noticed something on my arm and told me he wanted to do further testing on the arm. Well sure enough, later that day he called me and told me that I have a terminal illness. He wanted me to come back to the hospital.

Since I was fired, I no longer have health insurance. On top of that

When I was returning to the hospital I lost the lottery ticket. Talk about luck, it would just be my bad luck if someone found the ticket and it was the big winning one. O' Woe is me.

MY BLACK BEAUTY

Gee, how I miss her
Now that she is gone
It doesn't seem right
And I know that I'll mourn

We were together
For quite a few years
Sometimes I think of her
And shed a few tears

I gave her the best
Of all that I had
Nothing was too good
And now I'm so sad

She took my heart
With her beauty so rare
She took my heart
With her coal black hair

She looked just like her Mother
And what a rare sight
She was tall and slender
And for her, you would want to fight

But after awhile
She got bored
It cut to my heart
Just like a sword

She would go out at night
And not come back till dawn
I'd toss and turn
Wondering where she had gone

I guess there were others
Who loved her as well?
I guess there were others
She thought were just swell

She left for good the other night
And I haven't seen her since
Maybe one night in the future
I'll see her sitting on my fence

Boy, I miss that <u>CAT</u>

THE LEAF

At the beginning of the warm spring air, I begin to form and will grow to become a microscopic bud on that which will sustain me.

As the air gets warmer I develop into a full fledge adult shape.
My veins are prominent throughout my being.

Most times I become green and take on different shapes and sizes. During the warm summer I reach full adulthood and my features gives pleasure to many people and creatures.

Ah, but when fall comes I begin to feel old age and my metabolism starts to change. A metamorphose begins to set in and is evident by the change in my structure.

I start to change color and sometimes I become red or orange or yellow or gold. I can still give pleasure as people will travel to where I display this beauty to gaze upon me and behold.

As life ebbs from my body I feel myself become brittle and finally my color leaves me and is replaced usually by a lifeless brown.

I loose my grip on that which has sustained me through my journey in this life. The final blow is when I fall to the ground and am absorbed by mother earth from which I came.

A SPECIAL DAY

It's Valentine's Day again my love
And I am here to tell you
All the love I have in my heart
Is there for just one, guess who?

To you I pledge my love and life
And all that I hold dear
To you I pledge my life's meaning
And all that I hold near

For all the things that we hold close
No one can compare
And on top of that my love
I'll bet that no one will ever dare

No one even comes close
To sharing all my love
There is no other in this world
It's you my precious turtle dove

I wake up in the early morning
And I see your lovely face
I keep the vision with me all day long
As I go through life's rat race

When I'm working or having fun
All through the live long day
It's back to you that I desire
And I'll surly make my way

I listen to the love songs
Those others compose and write
To me my love and wonderful wife
They had you in their vision's sight

For all the sweet words in this wide world
None can really quite compare
To you my sweet darling
And that is being quite fair

To me my one and only love
None could ever take your place
I set my standards very high
And you are the one who won the race

And so I say to you my love
On this a very special day
You know just how I feel
And there is no more that I can say

AN ICEY WINTER

The swirling winds and bitter cold
Send shivers through my whole being

Then the snow comes and engulfs me
Like an ice cold shower or being naked in a freezing
running stream
I tremble and shake like a leaf caught up
On a tree in a hard wind

My soul is trembling to the very quick
There is no comfort to be found
For I am very poor
And to this life I am bound

I must travel and walk
During this bitter cold
In order to have some substance in order to sustain
my life
To the meager job that I hold

It wasn't always this way
But luck turned against me
When Lady Luck turns her back to you
You pay dearly, don't you see

Once upon a time I was riding high
And I had it all
Lady Luck slapped me in the face
And I had a hard fall

It's no fun, being so down
As you are always looking up
You see the distant fields of green
You want to be in the middle of it and hold the winning
cup

Every day you hope and pray
A better life will come to you
And you will do better
Some how, some way, something new

You must fight the winter squalls
To preserve your health and life
You must persevere
And fight all the strife

If summer would only hurry up and come
You wouldn't feel this winter's chill
Your situation wouldn't change much
You would want a better life still

It would not change your financial being
As you would still have to go to that meaningless job
But at least when you get there
You would not feel like a frozen door knob

ANIMALS

My little doggie
All black and white
He's so pretty
What a lovely sight

He cuddles by me
All day and night
He's a wonderful dog
He doesn't even bite

All he wants is love and care
So I give him what he needs
And a little extra at times
And he plays in the weeds

We also have a cat
As playful as can be
She's a little angle
As anyone can see

To watch them together
Rolling to and fro
It's a sight to behold
And I know it is so

They make my day
So full of joy
Just watching them play
And looking so coy

Animals can make your life
Such a pleasant thing
When you stop to think about it
They can almost make you sing

They bring such joy
In little children's hearts
Watch them playing together
It's such a wonderful start

AUTUMN

Where has it gone?
Those wonderful days of fall
Now we look out of the window
And try hard to recall

We would go for a walk
Along the trails in the park
We would stay out
Until it would get dark

It wasn't too cold
To go out and fish
Now all that we can do is
Look back and wish

It wasn't to cold
To go out and wash the car
Now we have to go to the car wash
This is now very far

We look at the flowers
In the back yard
They have withered and died
And looking at them is very hard

The leaves have turned
To orange, browns, and red
It seems like the plants
Have all gone to bed

The pool has been closed
For quite a while
The tools have been put away
And we have cleaned the tile

The chairs are all covered
With tarps of blue
We had to buy more
Because the old ones wouldn't do

Don't forget
To winterize the car
Because if you don't
You will not get very far

The neighbors are scarce
You don't see them much
They stay in the house
And move around in a rush

You have to buy food
And other things
It's real cold outside
And you wish that you had wings

On those cold mornings
You hate to get out of bed
You wish that it would snow so hard
You could go back and rest your head

But you must go to work
To pay your bills
If you don't have a car
You must walk those hills

If you are retired
And don't have to work
You are lucky
And that's no quirk

You have paid your dues
And don't have to go out
You can stay in your warm house
And don't have to shout

Warm weather is coming again
And you just can't wait
About this cold weather
You just have to hate

So I say to you
My good friends
Autumn is gone
As it always ends

BASEBALL

What a good day
To go to the park
The weather is warm
I'm happy as a lark

I'll take my son
To his first game
To make him interested
Is my ultimate aim

The park is new
And looking grand
The music is playing
By a ten piece band

The cotton candy and hot dogs
Are selling real fast
I have to wonder
Will they all last?

The players take the field
And the pitcher throws the first ball
It's hit real hard
And hits the far wall

The outfielder scrambles
To catch the ball
He runs too fast
And takes a big fall

The crowd screams
With a big sigh
The ball is thrown home
But it is too high

The runner advances
And goes to third
He passes second
As the coach is heard

My son is real quiet
As he takes it all in
He's routing for the home team
And hoping for a win

The game is real good
And goes as it should
Our home team won
As I knew they would

My son was happy
And I was too
We had a great day
Yes, wouldn't you?

BEAUTY

If you wake up in the morning
And have your health
Life is beautiful

If your spouse is by your side
Both physically and mentally
Life is beautiful

When you go to work
And enjoy your job
Life is beautiful

While at work
You get along and enjoy your coworkers
Life is beautiful

When you come home from work
And your family greets and loves you
Life is beautiful

When you work in your yard or anywhere
else
And all around you is beauty
Life is beautiful

When you are with your friends
And all have a good time
Life is beautiful

At the end of the day
And you relax at home
Life is beautiful

The beauty of life
Will always be
Beautiful

BEING ALIVE

To Be

To Live

To Have

To Give

To Play

To Weigh

To Smile

To While

To Eat

To Meet

To Run

To Sun

To Wish

To Fish

To Go

To Slow

To Meet

To Greet

To Beat

To Defeat

To Kiss

To Miss

To Pout

To Shout

To Break

To Repair

To Give

To Share

To Her

To He

To Compare

To Glee

To Reap

To Sow

To Morn

To Scorn

To Laugh

To Cry

To See

To Die

BIRDS

On a warm spring morning
I looked out of my window
And behold a wonderful sight
There were Robins on the ground
Resting from a long winter's flight

They were chirping and singing
And digging in the ground
They were looking for worms
And what ever else that could be found

Some are in trees
Building their nest
And some are on the ground
Making a mess

I don't really mind
As you can see
Because I really missed them
When winter came, and they had to flee

I live in the north
Where it really gets cold
They had to fly south
Is what I have been told

It's good to have them back
As anyone can see
Their chirping brings happiness
Especially to me

They are one of God's creatures
For all to enjoy and see
What would this world be,
Without them and others,
For you and I to see?

BIRTHDAYS

When it's that time of year
And the day is finally here
Do you look forward to it?
And expect things from your dear

If you are young or old
Or somewhere in between
You look for recognition
And want to be really seen

Did you get the present you want?
Or was it something you need?
Did you get a present at all?
Or only a card for you to read

Were you really good or bad?
And didn't deserve a thing
Is your birthday in the winter?
Or does it come in the spring?

Is it in the summer?
Or is it in the fall?
Maybe you just didn't deserve
Any present at all

But that's not the way you think
You think that you should get it all
You want presents in both your hands
And take away a great big haul

But it doesn't matter my friend
No matter how much you connive
The greatest gift of all
Is just being alive

CHILDREN

Children are a real joy
They give you pleasure
It's beyond belief
And beyond all measure

You watch them grow
Innocent of life
Sometimes they hurt you
And it cuts deeper than a knife

Most are very good
And don't disappoint you
A few turn out bad
And that is oh so sad

You hope for the best
That life can bring
You want them to do things
That will surely make you sing

You take them
To their first day of school
You just hope
They don't act like a fool

You worry
When they get sick
You do all you can
To help them to get well quick

They say and do things
That makes you laugh
Although they don't know it
They take you through your pleasure path

You do things to protect them
Regardless of what
You want them to be happy
And not live in a rut

Sometimes we want them to be
What we never could be
But they have to live their own life
And we'll just have to wait and see

CHRISTMAS TIME

It's Christmas time
Yes, that time of year
When we all gather
From far and near

We get together
To have some fun
Some of us are busy
And on the run

It's to the stores
Start in at dawn
Get the gifts
Before they are all gone

Something nice
For your spouse
Don't be cheep
Or they will call you a louse

Then there are the kids
With all the toys to buy
Make sure there are enough
So the kids won't cry

There are parties to attend
With some of your friends
Some are so good
You wish they would not end

Some go out caroling
With a small group
They try to stay warm
With cups of hot soup

Have you decorated the house?
With all the bright lights
Make sure the kids help
So there will not be any fights

Some take vacations
At this time of year
They like to go away
And not spend it here

Where ever you are
Don't forget the reason
Christ was born on that day
That's why we have the season

DID I THANK YOU?

Did I thank you today my Lord?
For all that you have done
Did I thank you, my God?
For giving us your son.

For it is through him, my God
That my life has changed
He has made me see the light
And now my life is rearranged.

I no longer do the things that I did
As I was in the dark
My life has turned around
And I am as happy as a lark

I try to do for others
As you would have me do
It is such a blessing
And it is all because of you

I see so many things
In a big different way
I want to do so much
And live by what you say

I am guided by you, my Lord
In what I say and do
It has made a difference
And all because of you

Did I thank you today, my Lord?
For turning my life around
Did I thank you God?
For making my life sound

In my hours of need
It is you in whom I seek
You can comfort me
When I am so weak

You give me what I need
To ease my troubled mind
My Lord and God, to me
You are so very kind

If I have not, my lord
Then let me try to start
Thank you so much God
And that comes straight from my heart

DID YOU SEE HIM?

Did you see him last night?
When you went to bed
Did you see him this morning?
When you raised your head

Did you see him in the bathroom?
When you washed your face
Did you see him in the kitchen?
Making breakfast in your usual haste

Did you know he was with you?
When you got in your car
Without him being there
You wouldn't get very far

He is always with you
If you like it or not
Try living without him
You will surly rot

The lord my God is everywhere
Looking out for us all
Have you not seen his miracles?
They are all so very tall

He is with us every day and night
To guide us along the way
He will pick us up when we fall
Regardless of what they say

I put my trust in my God
Who looks out for me from above
There is no other that I feel this way
I give him all my love

He has guided me this far in life
Who else has done so much?
I would not be where I am
Without his help as such

I hope that you know for yourself
What God has done for you
Above all else and everything
You must give him his due

FACTS

There comes a time in everyone's life
When we must face the facts
Putting it in front of us
Is like putting it in sacks

We reflect on what we have done
And this means the good and the bad
Others know how we have lived
And the bad is so sad

We want to have two sacks
The biggest being the good
The tinniest sack of bad
We try to shove under the wood

We cannot hide our emotions
They come to the surface like dirt
Sometimes they are good
And sometimes they can hurt

We want to impress all others
By the good things we do
Some people don't see it
And question and say, "Who you?"

In life there are mysteries
Far more then we know
It's how we handle them
It's how most will show

Do we want to be remembered,
By the things we did in life?
Will people say he was good?
And lived without any strife

FATHER LOGAN

Father Logan we want to thank you
For all that you have done
You have been a role model
In the battles you have won

You were there
When it wasn't fun
Many times we know
You were under the gun

You fought our battles
In our time of need
You stood your ground
And planted the seed

If it wasn't for you
In our time of need
There were things you did
For us to succeed

You have seen so much
In all of your years
You continue to comfort us
From all of our fears

You have followed God's teachings
In every which way
You pray hard for us
In the words that you say

You have led us to Christ
Through the things you have said
It will remain in our hearts
And stay in our head

We need God's blessing
In all that we do
It comes from someone
And that Father, is you

You have been a strong rod
Weathering the storm
You are there Father
Just keeping us warm

Through good times and bad
You have fought for right
With God in your corner
You never loss sight

No greater gift
Than the honor we give
To a man like you
And the life that he has lived

We respect and honor you
On this special day
We give thanks to God
As he wanted it this way

FEELINGS

Why do I,
Feel this way?
Is it love?
I dare not say

When I see you
My heart goes to pieces
I don't know why
But it just increases

This thundering sound
In my chest
Will not let my heart
Come to rest

All my friends
Know the reason why
They all tell me
I act like I'm high

You're like some flowers
In a garden of weeds
I just wish
I had planted the seeds

You make my days
And my nights too
I could not live
Without seeing you

And then comes the heart ache
By what you do
As there are others
Who pursue you too

I saw you with one
The other day
You spoke to me
And all I could say was, "Hey."

You just don't know
What you do to me
It tears my heart up
If only you could see

Yes, it's love
I feel for you
There is no other reason
And I admit it's true

Maybe one day
You'll return my love
Then we'll become
Like two turtle doves

FISHING

It's 4 in the morning
And I've got to get up
I want to go fishing
So I need coffee in my cup

I've got to be alert
For what I've got to do
Pick up my buddies
Crazy Joe and big Lou

We are going to the river
So I must hitch up my boat
I've got to make sure
That it will float

There's gas to buy
And some snacks too
Plenty for me
And plenty for you

It's a pretty far place
We've got to go
I've got to make sure the tires
Are just so

When we get there
At the crack of dawn
There are other boats
Sitting on the lawn

We wait our turn
To get in the water
We ease our boat up
Right to the border

We are finally off
To catch our prey
We'll be satisfied
With anything that day

We came home that evening
With a boat full of fish
After they are cleaned and cooked
They'll make a great dish

I'd rather go fishing
Than working at all
I do believe
That fishing is my call

FLOWERS

I see the beauty
In all the flowers
I can watch them
For many hours

There are the yellows
And the blue
Orange and reds
They look so true

I see the leaves
All shades of green
They are like this
Just to be seen

Some have fragrance
So sweet and clean
It temps your nostrils
To be real keen

Some are large
And some are small
I love the beauty
In them all

They must have water

In order to grow
Sometimes you trim them
Just to show

Some love shade
And some love sun
Does it really matter?
When all is said and done

We use the flowers
For many things
It makes us happy
From commoners to royal kings

In God's infinite wisdom
He put flowers here
For all to appreciate and see
Both far and near

FRIENDS

We grew up in the same neighborhood
And always remained friends
We did a lot of things together
And was the talk of the neighborhood's old
hens

Then we went our separate ways
And followed different career paths
We had different girlfriends
And made them our better halves

We traveled the world over
And did many things
There was not much we didn't see
Yes, I'm talking about you and me

Many years has past
And now we are getting old
I think about tomorrow
And know it can't be told

We have our aches and pains
And take so many pills
Regardless of what they say
We still want to climb those hills

We see each other once in awhile
At different place and affairs
We stop to look and greet each other
And watch the others stare

Oh how life has changed us
And made us grey old men
We can't do what we use to
So now it's the young men we send

You will always be my friend
Regardless of what they say
We have been through too much together
And all we say is, "Hey."

Last night I learned you had left us
And was at those pearly gates
I wonder if you would ask Saint Peter
Your friend is coming, and would he mind if
you waits?

GANGS

Boys on the corner
Acting like men
Pushing and shoving
Shouting like a hen

Nothing for them to do
So they act like a clown
If they had a job
They wouldn't be around

They get into trouble
Because that's their way
They don't listen to their parents
As to what they have to say

They feel the gang is the right way
In what they say and do
They have no respect
For me or for you

They break the law
Time and again
Sometimes they get caught
And sometimes they win

They steal and rob
From me and from you
Then they hurt us
And we can't sue

They get into drugs
And loose all reasons
They are high all the time
For all four seasons

Their life is not worth a damn
For man or beast
Is it worth saving?
To say the least

They are some ones children
And the parents do care
No matter what happens
They will still be there

But in the end
The law always wins out
They cry and moan
As the judge begins to shout

You can only hope
That jail will do them some good
They will be away for the drugs
As only they should

GOD'S GLORY

All of God's glory
Is here to see
Look around you
That's the key

See the birds?
In the tree
They are there
Because of he

See the flowers?
On the vine
He made them beautiful
Because he's kind

Feel the wind
In your face
It is there
By his good grace

Feel the rain
Upon your head
It would not be there
If you were dead

Does the sun shine?
In your face
Didn't you notice it?
In your haste

Why do the trees?
Grow so tall
They look up to heaven
And form a great wall

The bees pollinate
So many things good
God made it that way
Didn't you know that he could?

The food from the ground
God gives to you
He made it that way
I know that you knew

So in his glory
He gives to us
Use it wisely
And please don't fuss

HAPPINESS

Have you ever wondered?
What makes a person happy?
Have you ever looked in a child's eyes?
And saw the glee or listened to the happy
laughter?

Or have you ever heard the birds
Up in the trees early in the morning
Singing and chirping
Their melodic tunes?

Sometimes you can watch
A dog or cat play with a toy
For endless time on end
And watch the delight in their manor

If you give your love one
A present on a special occasion
And see how they look at you,
Or how they react, you will know

At times you may see a person sitting
Reading a book and have
That far away look in their eyes,
They are very happy

Go to an amusement park
And watch the people enjoying the rides
Or playing the carnival games,
They are extremely happy

Watch a young man
Tinkering under the hood
Of his first car
He too is happy

How about a young girl
Trying on her first prom dress
Don't you know,
The joy she feels?

Have you ever seen two old people?
Walking in the park
They both hold each other's hands
They are happy

Watch a mother
Nursing her first born child
There is so much glee in her expression
She is happy

Receive an award
For something you have done
You can't wait to show it to someone
You are happy

There is a strong correlation
Between love, joy and happiness
They are almost intertwined
All three are a state of mind

Are you happy?

HOLIDAYS

We're all here for the holidays
We come from near and far,
We traveled by bus and train,
And some came by car

Mom is in the kitchen,
Cooking just like mad,
Sis is in the bedroom,
Trying not to be bad

Dad is in the dinning room,
Looking for the knives
We just hope that,
He doesn't get the hives

My brother is outside,
Playing in the snow
He's making a big snowman,
And hoping the sun doesn't make it go

Grandma is on the couch
Taking a little nap
Grandpa is outside taping the maple tree
Hoping to get some sap

I'm in the chair, watching the football game,
Trying to see the score
Along comes the dog to play with me,
Will I be able to see more?

Mom tells us it's time,
To come to the table
I jump up and wonder,
If next year we'll all be able

Being with our family,
This time of the year
Is a glories event
To be with those, we hold dear

It's not always easy
To do the things we love
Some of our family,
Could be in heaven above

HOPE

Don't despair
There is hope
Without it
We couldn't cope

When I am down
And don't know what to do
I wish for something good
And know that it will come true

If that's not hope
Then tell me why
If you can convince me
I'll break down and cry

We all want something
Good or bad
We hope for it
Then we won't be sad

If it happens
That's really good
Most of the time it doesn't
And we wish that it could

We need hope
To keep us alive
Without it
We wouldn't survive

For what does it mean?
To become a shell
Without hope
We might go to hell

Sometimes we pray
And hope for more
But we never pray
And hope for war

We hope for our children
That they will do right
We want to see them grow up
And be a blessed good sight

We hope that our love ones
Will always be there
We don't want them sick
And give us a good scare

We hope for ourselves
That we will do well
And get ahead in life
And do just swell

MY HOPE

When I see the morning sun
My heart is full of hope
This is another day
And I know that I can cope

There are things for me to do
And places that I must go
There are people that I can help
And I must make it so

There's the man just down the street
Who has very little to eat
He lives alone and is very poor
He's the first one that I must meet

I take him groceries by the bag
And sometimes a pot of stew
I take him coffee by the pot
And hope that this will do

His wife died many years ago
And he still greaves for her
His memory is not what it use to be
And I still call him, "Sir."

We always have a cheerful talk
And he tells me about the past
So many facts that he forgets
But I really want it to last

Soon I must bid him goodbye
For there are others that I must see
There are so many people in this world
Who are less fortunate than me

I try to do whatever I can
For people that I know
For in this world we live in
We've got to make it so

We can't always cure the ills
That nature puts on us
But we should do something
And do it without a fuss

I go on my journey
For the rest of the remaining day
Trying to help those that I can
For God has made it that way

I NEED HIM

I close my eyes and there he is
Sitting by my side
I close my eyes and there he is
He will never hide

He is with me every day
To guide me with my life
He is with me all the time
Even through all the strife

I know that I need him all the time
Who else will see me though?
There is nothing that he can't do
I'll bet that you need him too

Trust in him in all that you do
He is always there for you
I cannot live without him
I'm wondering, can you?

I start my day by thanking him
For giving me my life
I end my day, the very same way
For giving me my wife

He has made me what I am today
A very proud man
Ask anyone who knows me
They will tell you, I'm his number one fan

No matter what I do in life
He will be with me
If you don't believe me
Just you wait and see

God is the one I speak of
Didn't you just know?
Trust him like I do
And he will surely show

I REMEMBER

I remember my first day at school
My Mother took me
And I thought
That it was real cool

Here I am
With girls and boys
I felt all grown up
And didn't have to bring my toys

Next came junior high
And I felt great
I met a new boy
And he became my playmate

Finally came high school
And I felt grown up
Little did I know?
That I was still a young pup

I went on to college
And that's when I knew
After meeting a nice girl
She was the one that I would woe

But then came the war
And I was sent overseas
Some nights in my fox hole
I couldn't even sneeze

The enemy was all around us
And we fought for our lives
Some of the young boys
Even got the hives

In the end we finally won
And I came back home
Everything was different
And I decided to roam

I hadn't been to many places
That I wanted to see
So I packed up my things
And left, my buddy and me

We traveled the world
And saw sights to behold
Heard many stories
Yet to be told

I'm now in my eighties
And all settled down
I did what I wanted
And look back without a frown

My life is all used up
And I don't regret it
I remember the things I did
And never did I quit

IN THE WOODS

I run across a babbling brook,
In the vast woods,
where I go to look.

The water is serene,
All blue and green,
Nature made it that way,
hard not to be seen.

As it cascades over some big rocks,
it defiantly reminds me,
of my little girl's locks.

Nature's creatures frolic all around me,
it is this beauty,
that I came to see.

The frogs down by the water,
jump to and fro,
they are watched by a deer,
and her little doe.

A rabbit stops to munch on the grass,
does he know,
how long this will last.

There are butterflies just landing on trees,
there are all kinds of insects,
just eating the leaves.

There are beavers in the water,
just building their huts,
there are squirrels all around,
just gathering their nuts.

I see the birds sitting up high,
if I could be with them,
I could reach up,
and almost touch the sky.

In one of the trees,
I see a big nest.
it is filled with bees making honey,
for all of the rest.

There goes a little red fox,
diving for it's hole,
it sees me and goes there,
to save it's hide and it's soul.

I see a little bear cub, running about,
where is it's mother?
so I dare not shout.

When I see life's beauty,
for us to behold,
I stop and think will it last,
as we get old.

We must take care of those things that are
here,
for if we don't, they will all disappear.
Then they will say, why and who?
and the answer will be you, and you, and you.

IN THE YARD

Well it's that time of year again
And you know what you've got to do
I'd better do it quick
Or hear yelling from my wife Sue

It's out in the yard
To cut the grass
Trim the bushes
Or they will not last

Fertilize the lawn
To make it green
Eliminate the weeds
So they can't be seen

Go to the store
To get some plants
Water them well
To keep away the ants

Get new flowers
To put in the ground
Plant them deep
So they will be sound

Set up the fountain
So the water runs well
Listen to the neighbors say
"Gee! That looks swell."

After you thought that you were finished
And relaxing with a beer
Your wife comes along and says,
"We've got more to do dear."

Well my friend, I say to you
What more is there for me to do?
I guess that you just don't know
My loving wife Sue

So you go along with her program
And work some more
While you do the work
She watches from the door

You just can't win
When it comes to the yard
Maybe next year
It won't be so hard

JUDGMENT DAY

When it is time for me
To leave this good earth
I hope that God and man
Will know my true worth

All of the things
That I've tried to do
To better myself
And live for you

I've followed your word
In my daily life
Doing the things
That would not cause strife

Knowing that I would
Be judged someday
For the things that I did
In every way

Knowing that my Lord
Would see it all
He would judge my life
And make his call

There are some bad things
I will admit
But when I realized it
I sure did quit

I feel that he forgave me
For all of my sins
If this is the case
I have all of my wins

I praise the Lord
Each and every day
For all that he has done for me
What more can I say

When I get to heaven
And I'm sure that I will
God will accept me
And I'll sit on that high hill

I do not fear my death
Or that judgment day
I know that I've done my best
There was no other way

JUST LIVING

As the waves slowly caress the bow of my boat sitting
in the dock,
It is like a kitten's paws kneading my stomach as I lay
on the bunk.

I listen to the sweet music of Miles Davis' "So What?"
and Shirley
Horn's, "All My Tomorrows." The melodic sound is
out of this world.

The euphoria is like floating on a cloud. Also, it is like
having an out
of body experience. The mild summer breeze blows
through to cool my body and brow. I think of nothing
but pure pleasure.

It was not always this way as I did not grow up with
a silver spoon in my mouth. I look out at the moonlit
vast sky, with so many stars and planets and wonder
is there somewhere just like this?

Is there someone or something wondering just like I am?
This is living, man this is just living.

JIMMY

As I lay in bed the other night
I heard a noise that gave me fright
And then in a soft voice it spoke to me
"It is Jim, yes this is he."

What a calming effect
It had on me
Yes, it was Jim
It truly was he.

My good friend
Had passed away
He was up in heaven
Where I wanted to be with him some day

He told me about
The beautiful things
He does all day
And how he sings

He is finally with his wife, "Reds"
Which he wanted to be
How happy they are
As every one in heaven can see

They watch over
Their Daughter, "Pat"
It doesn't matter
Where she is at

He does all the things
He ever wanted to do
He does them with
His wife and a guy name "Lou"

There is no tomorrow
There is only today
He doesn't try to rush
To try to make hay

He talks to God
Most every day
And tells him everything
He wants to say

He told me this is really paradise
Far out of my world
There is no way I could imagine
The glory that has unfurled

When I get there
I hope someday
He said that he has asked God
To please make a way

True friendship is always
Very hard to find
And prematurely
Jim left me behind

But I'm overly happy
For my friend "Jim"
There is no one here on earth
That could compare with him

LIFE IS BEAUTIFUL

Life is beautiful
When you go to school
You go there because
You don't want to be a fool

Life is beautiful
When you have a son
You love to watch him
As he has fun

Life is beautiful
When you have a girl
You sit and stare
As she plays with a curl

Life is beautiful
When you go to the shore
The days are all sunny
And you wish for more

Life is beautiful
As you watch your mate
And in your heart
You have no hate

Life is beautiful
When you have a good friend
You have no bridges to cross
And no arguments to mend

Life is beautiful
When evening appears
You sit on the porch
And have a few beers

Life is beautiful
When you go away
But it's always better
When you come home to stay

Life is beautiful
As you get old
You look back
And have your memories to hold

LIFE'S JOURNEY

In life's journey, there are up and downs.
We think of our childhood when it's all laid out for us.
We think only of what makes us happy.

Then comes the school years when life is only half
happy.
There is reading and studying to do. We can't spend
most of our time doing just what we want to do.

We are placed in a position where we must meet
expectations put upon us.
This is to fit in with society. These are hard days as
most of the time we would rather be doing something
else.

But to our amazement these days go by. We reach
young adulthood
and think that we know it all. We have no concept
that people older
than ourselves have lived and experienced far more
than we have.

For at this age if only we had the knowledge and
experience of these older people life would be so much

better for us. Ah! but I know now what I wish I had known then, I would have been so much better off. Life is like this. You have to experience things on your own to gain the knowledge for yourself.

For it is at this time of life that you begin to make a life for yourself, good or bad. The training that you received, or lack thereof, while getting to this point will shape the rest of your life. This is life's general rule but there are always exceptions.

It is at this point that one starts thinking about what they want to do with the rest of their life. Also, how they are going to accomplish it. Plans are made as to how they are going to reach their goal.

Some succeed and others do not. It is always better to have a secondary goal in the event you cannot reach your primary one. Then there is the question of family. Do you want one or not? Do you want it now or later? Is one forced upon you? Will you live up to what's expected of you? Do you put your plans on hold? Will you ever go back to your original plan? So many questions, so many answers.

Life goes on and before you know it, you are at middle age. Have you succeeded? Have you failed? Only you can answer these questions. Then comes a time when you look back and say to yourself, "Where has all the time gone?" For now you are a senior citizen and the one who has most of the answers for that young you, you wished for when you were young.

So life's journey for you was a blast and only you can say, "I had a hell of a time," Which was either good or bad.

LITTLE CHILDREN

Little Children
In the city
All the shootings
All the pity

Little Children
Being gunned down
Little Children
Waiting to be found

Little Children
Joining a gang
Little Children
On corners they hang

Little Children
On the street
Little Children
Beating the heat

Little Children
In the school yard
Little Children
Playing real hard

Little Children
Forgotten about
Little Children
Wanting to shout

Little Children
Parents working
Little Children
Evil lurking

Little Children
Being taken advantage of
Little children
Needing plenty of love

Little Children
Working in sweat shops
Little Children
Wanting to call the cops

Little Children
Of tender age
Little children
Working for a small wage

Little Children
Out on the ground
Little Children
Waiting to be found

Little Children
Out on a farm
Little children
Away from city harm

Little Children
Still a mystery
Little children
Do they know their history?

We do what we can
To keep them safe
They do not realize
They're still a little waif

LOOK AND SEE

My brothers and sisters
Listen to me
The way they treat us
Yes, don't you see?

It has been this way
For a long, long time
I won't take it no more
No, not on my dime

Get up my brothers
Don't you see?
What the man has done
Yes, to you and to me

He has made us a mockery
For the world to see
The way he has treated us
No wonder we flee
But the days of slavery
Are long, long gone
We are in the limelight
With the coming of the dawn

Look at all the things
That we have done
To make the world a better place
To live in, under the sun

There's not a single thing in this world
That we can't do
Take a look around you, name something
We've done that too

We've built this country
On the labors of our back
We didn't get the recognition
And that's just a well known fact

We are involved
In all of the arts
When we participate in the sciences, education,
and other things
We give it all of our hearts

In the world of sports
There is none better
We excel to excellence
Right up to the letter

So don't tell me that we are inferior
That's just a myth
You know in your heart
That we are far superior

Stand up my brothers and sisters
Let us be counted for the things we say and do
I'm very proud of who I am
I'm wondering, are you?

LOOKING AHEAD

It's that time of year again
When we try to look ahead
With the new year coming in
We want to stay out of the red

Of course we have our bills to pay
To make our life worthwhile
Then there comes the income tax
Which we know we have to file

The more we make, the more they take
It just doesn't seem fair
Don't they have enough money?
We sure do pay our share

The new year is upon us
And we look forward to what it brings
Let's hope that it is a good one
And our lives are filled with good things

The Lord will not forget us
If we just stop and pray
He will hear you
And all the things you have to say

Do not forget your fellow man
For he is human too
He may not be as fortunate as you
But he is a person, just like you

Do all that you can
For those that you love
As God will see it
From high in heaven above

He will reward you
When the time is right
He will not forget you
And keep you in his sight

Thus, I say to you
My good and true friend
God will stay with you
Until the very, very end

LOST LOVE

When I saw you in the park that day
It brought back memories of many years
I don't know how I did it
But I fought to hold back the tears

The things that we did, in the years gone by
And the memories of them all
I'll love and cherish every one
Until the very day that I die

We were young and so in love
With all the obstacles in our way
We fought through them and did survive
In spite of what people had to say

We lived together for a time
And tried to make it work
It was good I must say
Although sometime I was a jerk

You did your best I must admit
And I never did blame you
It was I who had to leave
And didn't see it through

You just don't know how hard it was
For me to have to go
You wanted me to stay with you
But I just had to say, "No"

It was never my intention
To cause you any pain
It was never my intention
To almost drive you insane

My situation was unique
And you know just what I mean
It's hard to leave your children
Oh! Such a horrible scene

I made my decision
Based on facts you don't know
Ask me about it someday
And I'll surely tell you so

We went our separate ways
And carved a life of our own
Most of it was good, I must say
But the hurt will not be known

We all have great regrets
This much is widely known
But when we looked at each other
Very little of it was shown

Well my good and true love
Life will surely go on
We'll look back at our lives
And remember the good times gone

MEETINGS

I go to the meeting
To see where we stand
I make my presentation
And get a big hand

The boss is very pleased
I've done my share
I've contributed to the Company
And now he is out of my hair

Come Monday
It's the same old thing
Try to make more money
So the boss can sing

Some at the meeting
Get dressed down
They look at the boss
And see a big frown

He says, "Everyone here
Is not doing their share
It's like some of you
Don't really care."

If we don't make budget
Things will be rough
For some of you
Things will be tough

There are bills to pay
And equipment to buy
If we can't turn out product
This Company will die

We need everyone
To give it their best shot
So go out there
And don't walk, but trot

And for those of you
Who work in house
You've got to pick it up
And stop moving like a mouse

The boss was angry
And showed his displeasure
When he gets like that
We all will be measured

We need these meetings
To see where we stand
If we all do good
We'll get a big hand

But if we find out
We're not up to par
Then we find out
Exactly where we are

We all need our jobs
To pay our bills
So we must do well
Or hit the hills

MEN

The purity of man's soul
Is shown by his needs
The purity of man's heart
Is shown by his deeds

The labyrinths of man's brain
To distinguish friend or foe
Goes a long way
To give him comfort or woe

The character of his being
For all to see
Tells quite a bit
Just who is he?

The results of his actions
Either good or bad
Tells about his mind set
And the thoughts that he had

Does he help or hurt?
His fellow man
Is it good or bad?
When he follows his plan

Does he know that his actions?
Speaks for itself
Is it meant to be?
For his health or his wealth

Man goes through life
For better or worse
Will he be blessed?
Or will he be cursed

Seek not ye
Who venture afar
For the closeness of your friends
Will never be on a par

What man envisions
Does not always come true
But live up to your ideals
Because they tell a story of you

So be true to yourself
And do not falter
Follow your dreams
And do not alter

MOTHER NATURES THINGS

The wind surrounds me, the wind surrounds me
In the middle of the night
The wind surrounds me, the wind surrounds me
But I will not take flight

The sun surrounds me, the sun surrounds me
In the middle of the day
The sun surrounds me, the sun surrounds me
It is time to do what I may

The water surrounds me, the water surrounds me
I sail my boat
The water surrounds me, the water surrounds me
And it keeps it afloat

The fire surrounds me, the fire surrounds me
How do I use it?
The fire surrounds me, the fire surrounds me
How do I make it fit?

The earth surrounds me, the earth surrounds me
I plant my field
The earth surrounds me, the earth surrounds me
My faith is sealed

All of Mother Natures things
Are here for me
All of Mother Natures things
Are for me to see

How I use them
Is up to me
How I use them
Is for all to see

MY BROTHER BILL

Look at him
If you will
He loved life
And couldn't stay still

He was always
On the go
Name the place
And he would show

He would try
Anything new
Whatever it was
He would do

Bill always had
An adventure's mind
He wanted to see
That certain sign

Could he do it?
Yes or no?
He sure would try
Maybe so

When he was young
Baseball was his thing
He loved to pitch
And made that ball sing

Then came the war
And he did his part
He joined the Merchant Marines
Which he loved with all his heart

He later joined the Army
And traveled quite a bit
But he couldn't stay still
So he decided to quit

Marriage was in the cards
And so he took a wife
Three children were born
And this consumed his life

He worked as hard as he could
To give his family his all
The thing that was important to him
He didn't want to see them fall

He was a good brother to me
He protected me in every way
I would listen to him
In most everything he would say

My physical protector he was
Always looking out for me
No one dared to bother me
If he was there to see

But later in life, as it always does
Your health becomes an issue
You have passed on my brother
And boy, I'm sure going to miss you

May your travel to the other world
Be oh so peaceful and calm
Silently I'll be saying
The Lord's 23rd psalm

MY COMPUTER

As I sit in front of the screen
I push the buttons but do they care?
I push the buttons
And then I stare

I get a message
Loud and clear
"You can't do that,"
Don't you hear?

I talk out loud
To glass and metal
I just hope that no one hears me
As I finally settle

Is this machine
Smarter than I?
I know the answer
And finally say, "Eye"

I go back again
And give it a try
I try for hours
And then say, "Bye."

A few hours later
I'm right back at my desk
This machine won't beat me
So I give it my best

I'm punching buttons
Up and down
And the keys are making
This awful sound

What did I do wrong?
In this case
What did I do wrong
In my haste?

The mystery of the machine
Is too much for me
So I call my friend
For him to come see

He comes over
The very next day
I tell him my problem
And all he says is, "Hey."

He goes to the machine
And makes a few strokes
It's like children
It's got to be coaxed.

It's up and running
In no time at all
All the funny sounds are gone
Just like the fall

I thank him a lot for what he has done
Come tomorrow
He'll be back
As sure as the sun

Well I guess we're at the mercy
Of those in the know
Gee but I wish
It just wasn't so

Why they make these things
So hard to understand?
Don't they know us old folks
Would rather write it by hand?

MY DREAMS

Will they see,
The joy in me?
As I sail from,
Sea to sea

To far away isles, lush and green,
With no one to stop me,
By being so mean

They did not want me
To venture so far,
For the friends I had
This was their par

But I knew in my heart
I had to go
And no one could stop me
Not even my foe

With the cool sea breeze
In my hair,
The ocean was calm,
And sailing was fair

The dolphins swam by me,
So elegant and great
They knew that I loved them,
And bore them no hate

As the sun set on me,
Night after night
I braved the big waves,
Without any fright

As the sun rose in the morning,
So orange and bright
I felt like flying,
And soar like a kite

When the first land was sighted
I screamed with glee
For this is my dream
And joy within me

It is an island,
So lush and all green
The plants and flowers were beautiful
Just waiting to be seen

I toured the Island,
But could not find a soul
I drink in the beauty, to
Fill my life's hole

When morning comes
And it is time to go
I feel regret
But know it is so

So back to the boat
I slowly go
To explore other islands
To see what they show

I'm living my dreams
And boy is it good
To do what I want
As nobody understood.

MY FAITH

Here I am
And here I'll stay
In God's house
I love this way

We are all related
In a special way
God has touched us
Is what they say

Do for others
All you can
Do not be afraid
And take a stand

Under our skin
We are flesh and blood
Don't you know?
You are really my bud

I feel your pain
In every way
Let God heal you
This is his day

Being together
In a spiritual way
Helps us heal
Our troubles today

Love your brothers
And sisters too
This is what God
Wants us to do

When we get to heaven
This is what we all want to do
God has made a promise
He will love you too

There may not be a tomorrow
In this world of strife
Give yourself to God
He will give you everlasting life

So I say to you
And I do believe
God has made a promise
He will not deceive

MY FLOWERS

Once upon a yesterday
I saw the flowers grow
Once upon a yesterday
Through the parks I could go

But now I'm confined
Only to my room
And watch the walls
As they loom

I've grown old
And I'm inflected
Very soon
I'll be evicted

To the nursing home
They will take me
Four more walls
I will see

In my youth
I grew flowers
I'd watch them grow
For many hours

Red ones, blue one
Pink ones too
All the colors
I'd grow for you

In the spring and summer
I'd sell my flowers
I'd stand on the corner
For many hours

I have no one
To care for me
I'm just too old
Don't you see?

But those days
When I had my flowers
I'd sell them for weddings
And many, many showers

Pretty soon now
They will lay me to rest
And someone will place
A flower, on my chest

MY FRIEND

You know not why
It happened to he
It just as well
Could have been you or me

He lived his life
So very well
There are many
Who are willing to tell

He raised his family
So very well
He did all that he could
And rose to the bell

He served his country
As he should
He never looked back
As others would

There were good times
And there were bad
He endured them all
And was never sad

We had a friendship
That was just great
We shared a lot together
And there was never any hate

What ever he had
He would share with you
He never complained
And always made do

There were days
When things went wrong
He would face them
With words and a song

He was always upbeat
And rearing to go
He never knew the meaning
Of the word, "No."

But there comes a time in life
When we all must slow down
And everyone knew
That Jim was heaven bound

He loved the Lord
In all his glory
And Jim could tell it
In many a story

God has a place
For a man such as he
And if we get to heaven
You will surely see

So I say to you
My good friend
I hope to see you in heaven
As this is not the end

MY LITTLE GIRL

I knew when she was born
And I looked at her
I could see great things ahead
But I knew not when, they would occur

I remember well
The first time she spoke
She called out my name
And that was no joke

She started growing fast
And then there was school
She out did the other kids
And proved she was no fool

We use to play
Sometimes in the street
Her girlfriend would join in
And that was real neat

As she got older
And started growing up
Books became her playmate
She was no longer a little pup

I remember those hard times
When she would study most of the night
Then she would rise in the morning
And still be a lovely sight

Then it was off to college
And I didn't see my little girl
But I still missed her
As she was my shinning pearl

On to graduate school
So she could get ahead
She was at the top of her class
Boy! What a point spread

She went on to do great things
But then I knew that she would
She is recognized by everyone
By doing all the things she could

In all of the things she has accomplished
Ours is still a love story
She never forgot her Dad
Regardless of her glory

So as you can readily see
No matter where she is in the world
She stays in touch with me
And will always be, "My Little Girl."

<u>MY PAINTINGS</u>

I look at the canvas, so pure and white
I wonder what it will be, the final sight.

Then I know, what I want to paint,
It will be something bright, cherrie, and faint.

I grab my brushes, all full of glee,
and anticipate the painting,
and what it will be.

I reach for my paints, and mix a few,
trying to get, just the right hue.

When I go to the board, and make a few strokes,
I'm ever so mindful, to please most folks.

The ideas come to me, furious and fast,
I hope that the objects will be bright and last.

I continue to paint, both day and night,
hoping the painting, will be a beautiful sight.

As time goes by, and I come to an end,
there is little thought that the painting will
transcend.

If my work, is as good as I know it should be,
A masterpiece will emerge, for all to see.

The beauty of it all, is not what I have done,
but what I can leave, to mankind and my Son.

For when we stop and think, just why we are here,
we want to make the world a better place,
where we can live, without any fear.

So I use my talent, the best that I can,
to give to the world, and my fellow man.

MY SWEETHEART

When I think of all the things
You have done for me,
My love for you will abound
For everyone to see

You have been my true rock
In good times and bad
You make me feel good
Even when I am sad

There is not a time in my life
When I don't think of you
From morning to late at night
About all the things you do

You perk me up
Just holding my hand,
I see the gleam in you eye
And know that you can

What else could I want?
But your love so true
It is this love
That keeps me from being blue

It is you my dear and only love
That makes my world go around
This might not sound true to others
But to me this is very sound

I could not live without your love
Not even for a day
You make the blood pump in my heart
That keeps me alive in every way

There is no greater love
Than what I have for you,
God in heaven knows
What I say is true

And so my love
On this a special day,
I pledge myself to you
In every kind of way

MY WIFE-MY LIFE

When first I saw your smiling face
I fell in love right then
I knew that I had to have you
It was just a matter of when

I made it my soul mission
To have you for my wife
I didn't know how or when
But I wanted you, in my life

It wasn't easy pursuing you
Because all the guys were there
They didn't know how persistent I was
Or how much I could really care

You would give me a big smile
To keep my hopes up high
But when I tried to pin you down
That's when you would say goodbye

I would come by your house
But I could not get in
You Dad would say, "She's not home,"
And I would wonder, where you had been

Then one day out of the blue
Things just turned around
You knew how much I cared for you
And our love began to abound

We made a life together
Through hard times and the good
But with all the strife
I knew that we could

We did a lot together
To make a real good life
But it would not have ever happened
Without you my dear wife.

So when they ask me
Has my life been good?
With you my darling
I knew that it would

And so I say to you
My princess and my wife
You have my undying love
For the rest of my life.

OUR B.B.Q.

Gather my utensils
From far and wide
Fire up the grill
Make it hot inside

Put the chicken on the fire
One side down
Watch it carefully
As it gets brown

Turn it over gently
To the other side
Some might be burned
That you've got to hide

When it's all done
Put it in a pot
When you serve your guest
You want it to be hot

Now comes the ribs
Stoke the charcoal hot
Put them in the fire
You know they'll eat a lot

Then there are the other things
You know you have to do
Get the beer and soda
Before you are through

There is potato salad and rolls
And maybe some pickles too
Get them all together
Before you can say you're through

You have to get some ice
To put in the coolers there
Then you have to decide
They are going to go where?

You have been working all morning
To have everything in place
You hope you haven't forgotten
Anything in your haste

But as you all know
To make everything nice
There's always something you forgot
Maybe it's the rice

Then here comes your company
Shining with the sun
They don't know what you have done
So they can all have some fun

And at the end of the day
When it's all said and done
There's no question about it
Every last one, did have big fun

OUR LORD

When morning comes
And you're all rested
Thank the Lord
In whom you trusted

When you went
To bed last night
You prayed to him
To keep you in his sight

He has brought you through
All kinds of trouble
He has been there for you
And didn't burst your bubble

For now you know
All his power
He looks at you
As his flower

There is nothing
That he can't do
Ask, and he will be there
Just for you

When you need him
Just say his name
He will answer
Just the same

I know the Lord
Is there for you and me
Just look around
Don't you see?

When this life
On earth is done
It is to him
That we will run

Trust in him
With all your heart
Don't you know?
He'll do his part

PEACE

By Ralph J. Taylor

I saw a bird the other day
As I was strolling through the park
This bird had many colors
But reminded me of a lark

As I sat down to eat my lunch
This bird sat down with me
It sang a song for the world to hear
And the other birds chimed in with glee

It reminded me so very much
Of the people of this world
If we tried a little harder
We could all become unfurled

There would be no strife
And no more war
Then man would have to say
What is the reason and what for?

We all could live in peace
And have no more fear
Of the untold things to come
Then enjoy ourselves with the things that are
here

I often wonder what it would be like
Not to have to worry
Could we live our lives in peace?
And not to have to hurry

Do we hurry because we know?
Life on this earth is not very long
We say and do all that we can
Sometimes we say it in a song

If we were to realize
The fruitfulness of it all
Those things that we worry about
Would seem so infinite small

If we could channel our energy
In just a positive way
Think of all the things we could do
And see what the world would have to say

So I say to you my friend
Just give it some serious thought
Then you would have to wonder
What was the reason that we really fought?

PLAYING MUSIC

As a little boy
Music was taught to me
I picked up on it
As you can plainly see

I started playing when I was four
And down through the years
I learned a great deal more

There were hours of practice
For me to do
Scales and rhythms
All to go through

And then one day
Out of the blue
It all came to me
Now I'm as good as you

I play in a band
Most every night
And practice by day
Until I get it right

But my greatest pleasure
Is playing for me
There is so much wonder
For all to see

When I'm in that groove
And feeling fine
Nothing can touch me
I've left mankind behind

I'm in my own world
With no one there
It's just how it is
And I really don't care

I don't know where it comes from
This improvisation I do
I thank it for being there
Yes, wouldn't you?

RAIN

As the rain falls
I close my eyes while outside
I let it penetrate my body
And soak my hide

There is something about rain
That has mystical power
I could stay in the rain
For many an hour

I do believe without a doubt
That it is angle's tears
That has built up
For many, many years

It penetrates your body
Right to your very soul
And if you believe
It will make you whole

Rain comes from the heaven above
It covers our seas and fields
I know this for a fact
And I also believe it heals

Without rain,
Where would we all be?
If we would never have it
Then you would really see

RETRIBUTION

Up in the sky I see an ominous dark cloud coming closer to me
As I look further I see my name imbedded. This freaks me out.
As the black cloud gets nearer, I see faces.

There is the cat that I drown when I was a little boy.
Then I see the little boy that I hit in the head with a baseball bat
as a teenager, because I wanted his toy.

I see the boys and girls that I abused as a young man.
Then I see the wife and little child that I abandoned.
They had to make it on their own.

There is also the grocer that I robbed and shot dead.
My life has just flashed before me and reminded me of all the bad things
that I did in my life. I shot him in the head.

A voice says to me, "Do you know what you did?", "Do you know what you hid?"

From my jail cell I look out the small window and it appears that the cloud is coming in to engulf me.

When it came in, there was more for me to see.
Oh how I regret and would love to just flee

But I know that the time has come for me to pay up for my transgressions. I must face the consequences and following sessions.

I hear the jailers coming down the hall for me.
All the other prisoners look out from their cells to see.

They will strap me in that chair and shave my head.
They will put the wires on and pull the switch.
I will shake and cry, until I'm dead.

My life is over
Far too soon
It is ended at midnight
In the light of a full moon

SHOPPING

Do you ever wonder why?
You have to go food shopping with your wife.
Can't she just do it by herself?
Doesn't she know that it cuts you like a
knife?

You hate to go through the isles
Getting bumped by the carts
Some ladies like to shop
Straight from their hearts

They don't care you have to stop
To pick up something from the shelf
They'll bump into you
So watch out for your health

I've got scars on both my knees
From shopping from some stores
Those carts really don't care
They'll leave you with some sores

And please don't try to get ahead
Of some ladies in a line
They'll knock you down and step on you
Then you'll really be behind

I tried to grab the last cantaloupe
Sitting on a stand
Some lady reached across
And smacked me on the hand

I guess she wanted it more than I
So I really didn't resist
She could have it for all I cared
It was not something I would miss

If I didn't love or have to eat
I wouldn't go with my wife
Then she would make it miserable
For the rest of my life

SNOW

When winter comes
And snow is here
You want to stay in the house
And snuggle up with your dear

You both will know
What you would rather not do
Go outside and shovel snow
Until you almost turn blue

She tells you to
Bundle up good
And you put on your jacket
The one with the bright red hood

The neighbors see you
And laugh out loud
When you look up
You see a big crowd

Oh! How you wish
Summer was here
Then you would be on the beach
With your wifee dear

But the hard part
Is still ahead
There are mounds of that stuff
So you shovel until you are almost dead

When you finally get through
And go back in
You get a phone call
From some of your kin

They tell you they are coming over
To help you shovel the snow
You are very exasperated
And tell them where to go.

Wouldn't you know?
You can't catch a break
Things are against you
And you ask, "Why, for heaven sake?"

I guess that I'll just relax
And have a cup of tea
More snow tomorrow?
I hope not, but we'll see.

SPRING

As I look out my window
This fine March morning
To my surprise
The snow was all gone

The air is still crisp
But I see the sun
It's going to be a great day
And I'm going to have fun

I love this weather
As it makes me feel good
Everything comes to life
As we all know that it should

The flowers start to bloom
And I feel so alive
I look in the trees
And see a new bee hive

There are buds on the trees
And the grass starts to turn green
All natures' things come to life
And wish to be seen

The children come out
And start to play ball
This is what they have been waiting for
Ever since last fall

I see my first Robin
Digging in the grass
It's looking for some worms
As it has done in the past

I know that the weather
Is going to get better
Although some days
It's going to get wetter

This will not matter
For the sun is sure to shine
There will be more of these days
This will leave the rain behind

This is my favorite season
Of all the four
Oh how I wish
There would be three more

SUMMER

It's Saturday morning
And it is real hot
We're going to the shore
And we'll take a lot

There's the big cooler to get
And load it with ice
Put in the drinks
And that will be nice

Make the sandwiches
And take the cookies too
Take the sun tan lotion
For the children, me and you

Get the bathing suits
And don't forget the hats
Pick up the towels
And add the mats

Then there is the umbrella
And take along the beach ball
Pile it all in the station wagon
For the medium long haul

Lock up the house
And put out the cat
Listen to the children
As they fuss and then sat

Stop to get gas
Along the way
Four dollars a gallon
Is what they say

It's getting real expensive
To go away
We're not going real far
And just for the day

We get to the beach
And look for a spot
Want to get near the water
Because it's going to be real hot

We have a good day
In spite of it all
We'll do it more this summer
Before the early fall

SWEET MUSIC

Have you ever heard,
A mellow voice so sweet?
You could listen all night
And fall at their feet

The song just touches your heart
And you mellow to the beat
It's so pretty
You can just feel the heat

It goes right to your heart
And melts your very soul
When you listen to it quietly
It just makes you whole

You want to sing or hum along
But you don't have the voice
You do the best you can
And it leaves your eyes so moist

You are so into the song
No matter where you are
You would rather be at home
But you are in your car

You pull over to the side
Because you don't want to loose your
composure
You might forget where you are
And commit yourself to exposure

You listen so intently
And wish it was you
Making such sweet music
And people would say, "Who?"

But then it's back to reality
And life takes a turn
You know that you can't sing like that
You have to go to work and earn

THE CABLE MAN

The cable man
Is due today
He will come on time?
This is what I pray

I have other things
I have to do
Everyone has
Don't you?

They said he would be here
Between 9 and 10
When he gets here
I know not when

I've waited before
For him to show
He came late at night
Wouldn't you know?

To my surprise
He came on time
This is a rarity
And blew my mind

He looked around
And got his tools
Laid them all out
According to rules

He played around
For an hour
Then he told me
He needed more power

He went back to his truck
To look for something
Then he came back
With this dumb looking thing

Tried to put it
On the wire
Said his boss
Was a big liar

It wouldn't fit
No matter how he tried
Then he told me
This shows, my boss lied

Then he told me
He'd have to come back tomorrow
Don't you know?
That was to my sorrow

I wasted all morning
Fooling with him
I missed my workout
At my local gym

And now again tomorrow
It's the same thing
I'll waste all morning
Waiting for the phone to ring

He called and told me
The part is on back order
The bad news is
It won't be in, until next quarter

Two days wasted
For a missing part
Doesn't the cable company?
Have a big, big heart

THE CARD

I sent you a card
This Valentine's Day
In it were words
I wanted to say

It told of my love
For you this day
It told of my love
In a special way

My feelings were vented
In an exceptional way
It just expressed
What I wanted to say

I wanted you to know
My inter-self
And how you give me
My inter-wealth

Without your love
I could not exist
Your love for me
I could not resist

You have made my life
Such a pleasurable thing
I have this inter-feeling
I always want to sing

I want to tell the world
All about you
And the many wonderful things
That you and I do

Being in love
With you my dear
Is like seeing the world
So very crystal clear

You make me so happy
Every day of my life
I am so glad
That you are my wife

No one, to me
Could be the way that you are
You are outstanding
And phenomenal, this by far

So I say to you
On this a special day
My love for you
Is true, in this special way

THE CITY BIRDS

When I go to the park
To get some rest
I look up in the trees
To find some birds nest

I like to hear
All the birds sing
It is a song of happiness
That they bring

It makes me relax
And feel so good
Just to hear them sing
As I know it would

I bring some nuts
For them to eat
I love to see them
Walking at my feet

There are Robbins and Bluebirds
And Pigeons and Crows
My love for them
Sure does show

I talk to the birds
When no one is around
I even whistle for them
When they can't be found

I hope they understand me
When no one is about
Sometimes I just whisper
But will never shout

Don't you just love them?
For the creatures they are
But don't get mad
When they poop on your car

THE FLY

I see the fly
On my table
I will kill him
If I'm able

He's been bothering me
For a few hours
If I kill him
I'll send him flowers

I swat at him
And I miss
He looks at me
And starts to hiss

He knows I want him
And flies around my head
If I catch him
He's as good as dead

He plays tricks with me
And hides from view
When I think he is gone
He comes back, right on que

He's the biggest fly
I've ever seen
I guess that makes him
Really, really mean

I have chased him
All over the house
He doesn't know
I'll catch that lousy louse

I won't give up
Until he's dead
My fly swatter will smash him
Right across the head

He's gone again
I know not where
All of a sudden
He's on my hair

I curse at him
And I'm real loud
I make so much noise
I draw a crowd

There he is
On the wall
I swat at him
And he does fall

I run right over
And step on him
He was so good
I called him Tim

But in the end
I got that fly
He won't bother me
Now, or bye and bye

THE GIRL NEXT DOOR

As I look at your smiling face
It stokes the embers in my burning heart
To a crescendo of heighten desire
That gives me a big start

A desire of longing
To hold and caress you
And also protect you
This I want to do

I have adored you from afar
For many years
I saw you when you were happy
And I saw you in your tears

It really hurt me to know
I was so close but also so far
By living next door I could see you
When you held your door ajar

Now that you have grown up
And can make up your own mind
Would it be too forward of me?
To ask if it is our time?

I don't want to hurt you
Or rush you too
But you should really know
What you want to do

I have been told
That you like me a lot
Could it be?
That you think I'm hot?

May I ask you out?
On a casual date?
This is one way
To see if we mate

To see you grow
From a little girl
You have turned into
A precious pearl

I really want you
To be my wife
I want to be with you
For the rest of my life

THE GOOD LORD

I heard the Lord
In the trees
He was there
With the breeze

I felt the Lord
With the sun
Even when
I was having fun

I see the Lord
In the sea
The waves are high
And so is he

He is with me
Day and night
He will never
Leave my sight

In all the things
That I might do
He is with me
To see me through

If you ask me
To praise his name
Be prepared
To hear his fame

He has saved me
From a life of sin
You just don't know
Where I have been

When things were bad
And I was down
He picked me up
Without a frown

I know the Lord
Is good to me
Can't you tell?
Can't you see?

He has given to me
More than I need
And to my life
He has the deed

Trust in him
In all that you do
Believe me my friend
He will come through

THE HEAT WAVE

It's hot outside
As you can see
The temperature is in the 90's
For you and me

It's a sweltering day
With no relief in sight
You think it's going to get cooler?
Well, maybe it might

The weather man said,
We are in a heat wave
I think I'd rather be
Somewhere in a cool cave

It's cooler there
And you don't sweat much
Take some water
Or anything cool, as such

You want to get away
From the city's heat
Put your feet in cool water
Boy, that can't be beat

But you have to work
To pay your bills
Why weren't you born rich?
Like the folks up on the hill

You come home at night
And sit on the porch
The heat is no better
And you still scorch

You open the windows
When you go to bed
Hoping for relief
For your sweating head

You are irritable as hell
And anything can set you off
It seems ridiculous
But even a tiny moth

You can't wait to get asleep
And get some peace
At least for a few hours
This misery will cease

Ah, but come tomorrow
It's the same thing
More heat predicted
That's all the weather man can sing

THE RAIN

Yesterday I saw the rain
As it came down
On my window pane

I went outside
To stand in the yard
It felt like I was in heaven
As it came down real hard

When I am out
In the rain
It washes away
All of my pain

God's waters
Has cleansed my soul
It drenches me
And makes me whole

I can stand there
Hours at a time
Thinking of poetry
And making words rhyme

I close my eyes
And hold my head high
Then you can hear me murmur
And let out a big sigh

I feel as if
The Angles know
How I feel
And how I show

My love for nature
Is second to none
I love the earth
And also the sun

The rain comes
And then it goes
When it will come again
Only God knows

THE WILLOW
TREE

Do you see that willow tree?
As the buds begin to open
This will be a good year
That is all I'm hoping

I planted this tree
When it was a baby
It will have gorgeous buds
Yes I know, well maybe

The leaves will be a deep green
And have a great shape
When they are all full
They will make a great cape

I'll look out of my window
Down by the lake
I'll see the branches hanging down
And the wind will make them shake

They will swing with the breeze
Gently back and forth
This is because the wind
Is blowing from the North

This tree will compliment
The flowers I've planted below
The reds, the violets, the blues
Yes, I know it is so

I'll remember my Mother
And what she said to me
That tree will bring you beauty
You just wait and see

And so I say to you
From the bottom of my heart
Plant a tree today
And give it a good start

It is a thing of beauty
For all the world to see
But even more than that
It means the world to me

THE WIRE

Where is the wire
That comes in the house?
Where is the wire, that's as quite as a mouse?

Where is the wire
That keeps me warm?
Where is the wire
That protects me from the storm?

Where is the wire
That runs the box?
Where is the wire
That's as strong as an ox?

Where is the wire
That heats my water?
Where is the wire
That I must order?

Where is the wire
That seems so strong?
Where is the wire
That can't go wrong

Where is the wire
That gives me pleasure?
Where is the wire
That keeps my treasure?

Where is the wire
That gives me light?
Where is the wire
That gives me sight?

Where is the wire
That cost so much?
Where is the wire
That I can touch?

The electric cords
That runs through the house
If I didn't have them
My spouse would call me a louse.

TOGETHER

They would not believe
What I said about you
About all the things
You say and do

I told them what you do every day
To make my life so good
It's not what everyone does
But maybe everyone should

It starts out with a morning kiss
That last all through the day
It's the special kind of kiss
That has a special kind of way

We embrace for a long moment
Before we go our way
There is something special about it
That will last us all day

In the evenings on cold winter nights
When there is nothing else to do
We snuggle by the fire
And read a book or two

Our love for good music
That plays throughout the house
As we both enjoy the sounds
Which are quiet just like a mouse

This might not seem like much
To most folks and you
But it brings us much closer
And our love will always do

There is a great gentleness
In our abundant love
It is like none before
And like two loving turtle doves

For when we are together
The world does not go around
It is like we are in suspended animation
And our love will not let us down

And so my love
If they only knew
About all the things I told them
Every one is so true

VACATIONS

Ah! It's that time of year again
We all look forward to
We can leave our bosses and jobs
And do what we want to do

Some will gather their families
And head out to the shore
Some will seek other things
And maybe do much more

The mountains seem real nice
This hot time of the year
Some will be going other places
Some far and some near

There are always the kids to consider
And what they would like to do
Have they told you yet?
What they want to do with you?

To plan a family vacation
Takes a lot of thought from you
It takes a lot of input
From everyone and you

And there are some independent
Who have no one at all
They go where and when they want
It's all a matter of their call

Vacations are nice to take
It frees up one's mind
To get away from the job
And leave all the worries behind

Vacations are over too quick
And it's back to the every day grind
Doing what you have to do
And leave all the fun behind

But whether you take them or not
It's nice to know they are there
I'll bet the family loves them
And that they really care.

VALENTINE'S DAY

It's Valentine Day again my love
So where do I begin?
To tell you how much I love you
And that is not a sin

I remember when we first met
And when we had our first date
I was so nervous
And didn't want to be late

I came to your house
And met your Mom and Dad
I hoped that they didn't think
I was just another cad

We went to the movie theater
And did enjoy the show
I didn't have much money
As my funds were very low

Then off to the park
To walk the long trails
To listen to the many birds
And their very sweet wails

Our love blossomed
And grew real strong
Together we meshed
Like a smooth love song

We have been together
For many a year
And through it all
I still hold you dear

I can't imagine, my love
What my life would be
Without you beside me
And I don't want to see

You are my anchor
That holds me close
And my love for you
Is more than most

Without you my dear
I could not live
Everything I have
To you I give

So to you my love
On this special day
I pledge my life and love
To you in a special way

WARM WEATHER

Summer is here
Don't you know?
Look around you
Doesn't it show?

See the flowers?
Beginning to grow
Warm weather is here
They sure know

Look in the trees
See the birds?
Hear them sing
Hear their words

See the stream
And the brook
As it runs
Around the nook

See the fish
Swim to and fro
The warm weather is here
They also know

See the children
Play in the street
Look real close
Boy, that's neat

They play ball
All day long
And they sing
A melodic song

The swimming pool is open
For all to go
You can cool off
Don't you know?

Ah! But for us grownups
It's a different song
Sometimes it seems
Summer stays too long

It's cutting the grass
And painting the house
A million things to do
So you don't feel like a louse

Washing the windows
Putting up the screens
Trying to get out of work
By any and all means

Then there is vacation
To think about
Where to go
And where to shout

Money is short
And not like it use to be
I guess we'll go to the shore
And enjoy the sea

The kids will be happy
Just to get away
They won't worry
They don't have to pay.

It's fun for all
Just to be together
For our two weeks
And just enjoy the weather

Then it's back to work
For another year
Try to save some money
So the family won't fear

WHERE HAVE THEY GONE?

Where have they gone?
Those years of mine
I speak of the good and the bad
Alas, my friend, now they are all behind

As a child I played a lot
And never thought of time
Things were good and never bad
I had no reason to whine

Then came the years when there was school
And I studied real hard
I wanted to make something of my life
And I would not be jared

My middle years went by real fast
And I still did real well
I raised a family, of which I'm proud
And they all turned out just swell

I accomplished the things
I really wanted to do
I have no regrets
Who would, would you?

There comes a time in everyone's life
When you have to look back and see
The good and the bad of what you did
And you ask yourself, "Who me?"

There's an old saying, "Time waits for no one."
And that includes you
What you make of time
Is a reflection of just what you do

You will be remembered
By those things that you did
Will they all be in the open?
Or will some of them be hide?

As you approach the golden years
You reflect on the years gone by
Are there some things that you would like to change?
Even some little white lies

We all know that it's just a matter of time
When we will met our maker
We just hope that he sees
We are not just another faker

Your life goes by so very very quick
And we can't live it over
So do the very best that you can
And live your life in clover

WINTER

When old man winter comes
I feel the icy chill
There are things that I must do
Even though it is against my will

There are windows and doors to seal
to keep the cold air outside
there is wood and logs to bring in
for a fire to warm my hide

I have to look for ice scrapers
To keep my car windows clean
If I don't do this, I'll have a bad accident
And cause a nasty scene

Somehow I hope my children
Will go out and shovel the snow
Whenever they get there
They will just play, this I know

When I put my cloths and boots on
To do this horrible task
I just hope it snows no more
This is all I ask

By the time I shovel my car out
And put the snow in the street
Along comes a snow plow
And pushes it back at my feet

If I could catch that driver
And tell him what I think
I would be so angry
I'd throw him in the drink

So I just grab my shovel
And do it all over again
There are days just like this
When you just can't win

I go back inside the house
and fix myself a drink
I sit down in my easy chair
So that I can relax and think

Life is not always pleasant
There are ups and downs
Do you think that everything is smooth?
Without any hills and mounds/

YEARS END

Where has it gone?
This past year
All the memories
That we hold dear

First it was New Year's Day
And the party we attended
We saw old friends
And it was splendid

Then there was spring
And getting the garden in order
Around the flower bed
We put in a new border

When summer came
And it got hot
There were so many things to do
And we sure did a whole lot

Autumn was upon us
Before we knew it
We went to movies and shows
And they were all a big hit

We got the kids and grandkids
Ready to go back to school
Buying new things for them
And that was real cool

Then came the winter
And all the snow
That's why I say
Where did the year go?

But it is nice to know
We still have good friends
We wouldn't trade it
And hope that it never ends

And so I say to you
Enjoy every day
Live it to the fullest
There is no other way

YEARS GONE BY

They are gone now
Those youthful years
As I look back
I shed no tears

They were good to me
Don't you see?
They won't come again
I just let them be

I look back
And reminisce
I remember the good times
Yes, those I really miss

Remembering my life
And all that I did
Some were good things
And some things I hid

Doing what was right
Those things taught to me
I learned my lessons
This I hope you can see

Going through life
Doing the right thing
Fills you with pride
And makes you sing

Having someone
Look up to you
Makes you proud
Of what you do

The lessons I've learned
I want to pass on
To someone younger
Who is facing a new dawn

If I can impart
The things that I know
When I reach heaven
They surely will show

So as you can see
My youth has passed me by
I often look back
And give a thankful sigh

I wouldn't trade it
For silver or gold
These are the treasures
That I'll always hold

YOU ARE GONE

In my mind I see your smiling face
It makes me want to cry
The last time I saw that smile
Is when you told me goodbye

I worshiped you in the morning
I worshiped you at night
I worshiped you so much
Sometimes I even have to fight

You went away and left me
Without saying a word
I didn't know that you were gone
Until on the street, I heard

Was I not a good lover,
To meet your every need?
Did I not tell you,
When it was time to heed

I did all that I could
To help you through the day
I did all that I should
To help show you the way

Maybe it was not enough
But it was all that I had
And now you have left me
And you leave me so awful sad

There will be another
To share this love with me
Just when, I don't know
I'll just have to wait and see

In life there are disappointments
Of this I am sure
Maybe my next love
Will not cut me right to the core

YOUR SOUL

You don't have to be hip
To have a lot of soul
You don't have to sway to the music
To be a part of the fold

Soul is a state of being
Within one's self
It is what makes you whole
And has nothing to do with your health

Have you ever stood in the shower,
Closed your eyes and pondered?
While the water cascaded over your body
And your mind just wandered?

Does it feel like the water is penetrating,
Through your blood, your organs, and your bones?
You have reached your inter self
And ask, "Is this the outer zone?"

If you do my friend
Then you are in touch with your soul
Stay for awhile
And it will make you whole

Do you see another image?
Is it whole and good?
Is this who you want to be?
And be this, if you could?

Does the image surprise you?
Do you wonder if it's you?
Is it really your soul?
If not, then really who?

Well my friend, I have news for you
It's not the earthly things that make up your soul
It's the things you do and the character of your being
That's the essence, that's who

When you leave this earth
And it's time to go
Do you wonder if your soul precedes you,
Or stays behind as it is so slow?

It is what you make it
Right here on this earth
Is it good or bad?
And what will heaven say it's worth?

Will your soul be going to heaven?
Or will it be going to hell
The answer is heaven
If you have done well.

YOUR WORTH

Your worth is determined by
What you did or didn't do in life

The smiles or lack thereof
You receive is also based on your worth

Did you try to achieve all that you could?
Or did it matter to you and your love ones?

Do we judge our status in life by what we believe?
Or what others believe?

Is there not a norm?
And do we not try to rise to it?

Those of us that truly care
Want to fit in with society and do well

Those that do not care are the ones that become
Non conformist and create problems for others

Would not life be so much better?
Without those who create most of the problems we
face?

Are we not our brother's keepers?
And does it not behoove us to try to reach back
And help those less fortunate than us?

And so I say to you my brothers and sisters
Do not become so aloft that you cannot reach out a
helping hand
To make someone's life a little better

We know that some don't want our help
But don't let that stop you

There are many that do
To give them the experience and advice of our
lifetime
Might just chance the world

YOUTH

Where have you gone,
Oh youth of mine?
Is getting old,
A fatal sign?

All the things
I use to do
Like jumping rope
And anything new

I can not do
Them quite as well
I'll fall down
And my knees will swell

Getting up
Is really hard
It is not as easy
As my body has been jarred

I'll go inside
And rub them down
They will feel like new
But only for a few

That night in bed
The pain will start
I won't be able to sleep
As it goes all the way to my heart

I guess tomorrow
To the doctor I'll go
There is another bill
But it must be so

Where are those days
When we would play in the dirt
And it didn't matter
Because we wouldn't get hurt

As the body ages
And the tissues get meeker
We can't take what we use to
As we get much weaker

Oh how I wish
I was a teenager once more
Then my body wouldn't ache
All the way to the core

WHY?

Why do we worry?
What tomorrow brings
Don't you know?
You can't change things

Why do we worry?
What our children do
Is it because?
Someone will sue

Why do children worry?
When Santa Clause is coming
They run around the house
And you can hear them humming

Why do we worry?
When the rent is due
Do we have the money?
Some from me and some from you

Why do parents worry?
When we are growing up
Do they have enough food?
For us to have sup

Why do we worry?
When the dog is barking in the yard
Is someone trying to break in our house?
Well, that won't be very hard

Why do we worry?
When we don't have enough clothes
I hardly have enough
To buy a decent pair of hose

Why do we worry?
When we are at work
Do my fellow workers,
Think that I am a jerk?

Why do we worry?
When friends stop by
Is my house that dirty?
That they can't come in and say, "Hi."

As you can see
We worry about everything
Wouldn't it be nice?
Instead of worrying, we would just sing